contents

Chocolate tips & tricks

Stir melting chocolate gently between bursts of microwave power

Ensure the base of the container holding the chocolate does not touch the hot water

One of the best things about these recipes (besides being both wicked and indulgent) is that they're not difficult to make. With a little background to start you on the right track and some helpful tips to keep you on the road to success, the trip to presenting an impressive and delicious fondue, cake, biscuit or dessert to an appreciative audience can be an enjoyable, and easy, journey.

melting chocolate

Please note that melting and tempering chocolate is not the same thing. Tempering chocolate subjects it to specific temperatures and techniques which result in the particular texture and sheen seen in fine chocolate sweets and pâtisserie.

Melting chocolate is not difficult if you follow a few rules. Everything you use when melting chocolate, from the pan to the stirring spoon to your hands, must be absolutely dry: the slightest amount of water in the chocolate will cause it to seize, that is, clump and turn an unappealing grey colour. Even an extremely humid day can affect the results. The second problem in melting chocolate is excessive or direct heat. No matter what method you choose to melt chocolate, patience and following directions are the two most important guidelines. Don't cut corners to save time.

Microwave-oven method

Place coarsely chopped chocolate in a small microwave-safe bowl; heat on MEDIUM power (55%), for 15- to 20-second intervals, pausing to stir gently between times. The chocolate will hold its shape even after it's melted, so the stirring is important. When the chocolate is almost melted, remove from the microwave oven and allow it to sit a minute or two to complete the melting process.

Stovetop method

This method takes more time but there is less to do than if using the microwave-oven method. Place a little water in a small saucepan – make sure the water won't touch the bottom of your choice of small heatproof bowl (a glass or china bowl is best) when it is fitted inside the pan. Cover pan and bring the water to a boil. Remove lid from pan; sit bowl,

Making chocolate curls

• Using a sharp vegetable peeler, scrape along the side of a long piece of room-temperature eating-quality chocolate (pictured left).

• For larger curls (above), spread melted chocolate evenly and thinly onto clean flat oven tray, cutting board or, ideally, a piece of marble; stand until just set but not hard. Scrape a flat knife across chocolate, pulling curls off with every movement.

• If the curls start to resemble shavings, the chocolate is too cold. Curls can be stored in an airtight container at room temperature until required (if the weather is hot, keep them in the refrigerator).

grating chocolate

Be sure that the piece of chocolate you intend to grate is chilled and firm. Grate on hand grater, cleaning the grater often so that the chocolate doesn't clog the surface of the blade. You can also 'grate' chocolate in a blender – this is especially recommended if you're grating a lot of chocolate – but be sure to chop the chocolate coarsely first.

uncovered, over the simmering water until chocolate is melted, stirring from time to time. After chocolate has melted, carefully remove the bowl of chocolate and wipe underside of the container with a dry tea-towel.

How to store chocolate

Chocolate should be stored in cool, dry conditions; if it becomes too warm, the cocoa butter rises to the surface and forms a slightly grey film known as 'bloom'. This is not harmful and, once the chocolate is melted, it will usually return to its natural deep-brown colour.

• If chocolate is refrigerated or frozen, bring it to room temperature before using.

• You will soon discover that chocolate is very sensitive to temperature change and you have to always keep the weather, room temperature, the heat from your hands, etc., in mind when dealing with chocolate.

Chocolate fondues

Traditionally, a fondue is served in a single pot that sits in the middle of the table. Provide your guests with skewers, then watch them dip piece after piece of fruit, biscuit, cake or marshmallow into the chocolate pot – this will prove a very popular way to finish the meal!

There are many different dippers that are wonderful for a chocolate fondue. Almost any fruit is suitable for dipping, as well as dried fruits, cake, biscuits, pastries, sweet breads and breads – just make sure that everything is cut into bite-size pieces and remember to remind your guests no double dipping!

Popular fondue dippers

- strawberries
- grapes
- cubes of melon
- slices of banana
- kiwi slices
- cherries

- orange or mandarin segments
- apple or pear slices
- fresh pineapple chunks
- dried apricots
- dates or figs
- dried mango strips.
- marshmallows
- biscotti (pages 22–7)
- cookies – bake them as a bar cookie and cut them into slices (pages 30–8)

- plain biscuits
- gingerbread
- pieces of plain butter cake
- brownie chunks
- panettone
- bite-size pieces of doughnut
- bite-size pieces of croissant
- shortbread
- pistachio bread (page 20)

You can also serve your guests small bowls of garnishes to dunk their chocolatey dippers in, such as chopped nuts, coconut or hundreds-and-thousands (always a hit with the children).

Fondues

caramel fondue with fresh fruit

preparation time 5 minutes cooking time 5 minutes

½ cup (110g) firmly packed brown sugar
⅔ cup (160ml) double cream
50g butter
250g strawberries, halved
2 medium bananas (400g), sliced thickly
2 small pears (360g), sliced thinly

1 Combine sugar, cream and butter in small saucepan.
Cook, stirring, until sugar dissolves and butter melts; bring
to the boil. Reduce heat; simmer, uncovered, 3 minutes.
2 Remove from heat; pour into warmed fondue bowl before
serving with fresh fruit.

serves 4
tips This recipes makes 1 cup (250ml) sauce.
The sauce is suitable to freeze.

white chocolate fondue

preparation time 10 minutes **cooking time** 5 minutes

180g white chocolate, chopped coarsely
½ cup (125ml) double cream
1 tablespoon Malibu
1 cup (130g) strawberries
1 large banana (230g), chopped coarsely
150g fresh pineapple, chopped coarsely
8 slices (35g) pistachio bread (see page 20)
16 marshmallows (100g)

1 Combine chocolate and cream in small saucepan, stir over low heat until smooth; stir in liqueur. Transfer to warmed fondue bowl.
2 Place fondue in centre of dining table; serve remaining ingredients on a platter.

serves 4
tips Fondue can be served with any of your favourite fruits. Malibu is the brand name of a rum-based coconut liqueur.

toblerone fondue

preparation time 5 minutes
cooking time 5 minutes

200g Toblerone, chopped coarsely
½ cup (125ml) whipping cream
1 tablespoon coffee-flavoured
   liqueur

1 Stir Toblerone and cream in small saucepan until smooth. Remove from heat; stir in liqueur. Transfer to warmed fondue bowl.
2 Place fondue in centre of dining table; serve with fresh fruit and biscotti.

serves 6
tip We used Kahlúa for this recipe but you can use any coffee-flavoured liqueur you like.

chocolate orange fondue

preparation time 5 minutes
cooking time 5 minutes

150g dark chocolate, chopped
⅔ cup double cream
1½ tablespoons Cointreau or
   orange juice

1 Melt chocolate in heatproof bowl over pan of boiling water.
2 Gradually stir in cream and liqueur. Transfer to warmed fondue bowl.
3 Serve fondue with fresh fruit, almond biscuits (page 28) or biscotti (pages 22–7).

serves 4
tip Cointreau is an orange-flavoured liqueur.

butterscotch & white chocolate fondue

preparation time 10 minutes (plus standing time)
cooking time 10 minutes

1 cup (200g) firmly packed brown sugar
⅓ cup (115g) golden syrup
50g butter
300ml double cream
100g white eating chocolate, chopped coarsely

1 Combine sugar, golden syrup, butter and cream in medium saucepan, stir over heat until sugar dissolves and butter melts; bring to a boil. Boil, uncovered, 1 minute. Remove from heat; cool 5 minutes.
2 Add chocolate; stir until smooth. Transfer to warmed fondue bowl. Stand 10 minutes before serving.

tips Serve this fondue with the fresh fruit of your choice. We particularly like banana, kiwi fruit, pear, apple and strawberries. The cream mixture must be cooled for 5 minutes before adding chocolate to avoid the chocolate 'seizing', that is, becoming grainy and firm and having the appearance of a dull paste.

serves 6

orange butterscotch fondue

preparation time 20 minutes cooking time 10 minutes

⅔ cup (150g) firmly packed brown sugar
25g butter
⅔ cup (160ml) double cream
1 teaspoon finely grated orange rind
2 tablespoons orange juice
100g white eating chocolate, chopped coarsely
1 large banana (230g), chopped coarsely
250g strawberries, halved
2 small pears (360g), chopped coarsely
2 medium mandarins (400g), segmented
18 marshmallows (110g)

1 Stir sugar, butter, cream, rind and juice in medium saucepan until sugar dissolves; bring to a boil. Boil, uncovered, 3 minutes. Remove from heat; cool 5 minutes.
2 Stir in chocolate until fondue mixture is smooth; stand 5 minutes. Transfer to warmed fondue bowl.
3 Arrange fruit and marshmallows on serving platter; serve with fondue and skewers for dipping.

serves 6

Just for dipping...

tropical fruit skewers
with orange glaze

preparation time 20 minutes **cooking time** 15 minutes

1 teaspoon finely grated orange rind
¼ cup (60ml) orange juice
2 tablespoons brown sugar
2 medium bananas (460g)
250g strawberries
600g piece pineapple
1 starfruit (160g)

1 Combine rind, juice and sugar in small saucepan; stir over low heat until sugar dissolves. Cool.
2 Preheat grill.
3 Peel bananas; slice thickly crossways. Hull and halve berries. Peel pineapple; cut into chunks. Slice starfruit thickly.
4 Thread fruits, alternately, onto skewers. Place skewers on oven tray lined with baking parchment; pour orange mixture over skewers, coating all fruit pieces.
5 Grill skewers, turning occasionally, about 10 minutes or until browned lightly. Serve with fondue.

serves 4
tips You need about half a medium-sized pineapple (1.25kg) for this recipe. Soak eight 20cm-long wooden skewers in water for one hour before using to prevent them from splintering or scorching during cooking.

fruit skewers

preparation time 30 minutes cooking time 10 minutes

½ medium pineapple (625g)
2 large oranges (600g)
250g strawberries
2 large bananas (460g)
30g butter
¼ cup (55g) firmly packed brown sugar
1 tablespoon lemon juice

1 Peel pineapple half; cut away and discard core. Cut pineapple into 2.5cm lengths; cut lengths crossways into 3cm pieces. Peel oranges thickly to remove bitter white pith; separate orange segments. Remove hulls from strawberries; cut in half crossways. Peel bananas; cut into 3cm slices.
2 Thread fruit, alternating varieties, onto twelve 20cm wooden skewers; place on oven tray.
3 Combine butter, sugar and juice in small saucepan over low heat, stirring until butter melts and sugar dissolves. Pour butter mixture over skewers, making sure that all fruits are coated in mixture.
4 Cook skewers, in batches, on heated lightly greased grill plate (or grill or barbecue) about 5 minutes or until browned lightly.
5 Serve skewers with fondue.

serves 4
tip You need twelve 20cm wooden skewers for this recipe; soak them in cold water before using to prevent them from splintering when you thread on the fruit and to stop them from scorching when being cooked.

pistachio bread

preparation time 10 minutes (plus standing time)
cooking time 45 minutes (plus cooling time)

3 egg whites
⅓ cup (75g) sugar
¼ teaspoon ground cardamom
1 teaspoon finely grated orange rind
¾ cup (110g) plain flour
¾ cup (110g) shelled pistachios

1 Preheat oven to moderate. Grease 8cm x 26cm slice tin; line base and sides with baking parchment, extending parchment 2cm above long sides of tin.
2 Beat egg whites in small bowl with electric mixer until soft peaks form. With motor operating, gradually add sugar, beating until dissolved between additions. Fold in cardamom, rind, flour and nuts; spread bread mixture into prepared tin.
3 Bake in moderate oven about 30 minutes or until browned lightly; cool in tin. Wrap in foil; stand overnight.
4 Preheat oven to low.
5 Using a serrated or electric knife, cut bread on an angle into 3mm slices. Place slices on ungreased oven trays. Bake in low oven about 15 minutes or until dry and crisp; turn onto wire rack to cool.

makes 35 slices
tips Uncut bread can be frozen after the first baking.
After the second baking, bread slices can be stored up to 4 days in an airtight container.
For a different spiced version, substitute the cardamom with ½ teaspoon ground cinnamon and ¼ teaspoon ground nutmeg.

lemon & pistachio biscotti

preparation time 20 minutes (plus refrigeration time)
cooking time 40 minutes (plus cooling time)

60g butter, chopped coarsely
1 cup (220g) caster sugar
1 teaspoon vanilla essence
1 tablespoon lemon rind
4 eggs
2¼ cups (335g) plain flour
1 teaspoon baking powder
½ teaspoon bicarbonate of soda
1 cup (150g) shelled pistachios,
   chopped coarsely
2 tablespoons caster sugar, extra

1 Beat butter, sugar, essence and rind in medium bowl until just combined. Add three of the eggs, one at a time, beating until combined between additions. Stir in flour, baking powder, soda and nuts. Cover; refrigerate 1 hour.

2 Knead dough on lightly floured surface until smooth but still sticky. Halve dough; shape each half into a 30cm log. Place each log on greased oven tray. Combine remaining egg with 1 tablespoon water in small bowl. Brush egg mixture over logs; sprinkle thickly with extra sugar.

3 Bake, uncovered, in moderate oven about 20 minutes or until firm; cool on trays.

4 Using serrated knife, cut logs, diagonally, into 1cm slices. Place slices on ungreased oven trays.

5 Bake, uncovered, in moderately low oven about 15 minutes or until dry and crisp, turning halfway through cooking; cool on wire racks.

makes 60

aniseed biscotti

preparation time 40 minutes (plus refrigeration time)
cooking time 1 hour (plus cooling time)

125g unsalted butter
¾ cup (165g) caster sugar
3 eggs
2 tablespoons brandy
1 tablespoon grated lemon rind
1½ cups (225g) plain flour
¾ cup (110g) self-raising flour
½ teaspoon salt
125g blanched almonds, toasted, chopped coarsely
1 tablespoon ground aniseed

1 Cream butter and sugar in large bowl; add eggs, one at a time, beating well after each addition. Add brandy and rind; mix well. Stir flours and salt into butter mixture.
2 Stir nuts and aniseed into dough; refrigerate, covered, 1 hour.
3 Halve dough; shape each half into a 30cm log. Place on greased oven tray.
4 Bake, uncovered, in moderate oven 20 minutes or until lightly golden brown; cool on trays.

5 Using serrated knife, cut logs diagonally into 1cm slices. Place slices on ungreased oven trays.
6 Bake, uncovered, in moderate oven about 25 minutes or until dry and crisp, turning halfway through cooking; cool on wire racks.

makes 40

mocha hazelnut biscotti

preparation time 20 minutes cooking time 45 minutes (plus cooling time)

1¼ cups (185g) hazelnuts
3 eggs
½ cup (100g) firmly packed brown sugar
½ cup (110g) caster sugar
1½ cups (225g) plain flour
1 cup (150g) self-raising flour
⅓ cup (35g) cocoa powder
2 teaspoons instant coffee powder
2 tablespoons Frangelico liqueur
100g dark chocolate, grated finely

1 Preheat oven to moderate. Spread nuts in single layer on baking tray; bake in moderate oven about 5 minutes or until the skins begin to split. Rub nuts firmly in clean tea towel to remove skins.
2 Beat eggs and sugars in medium bowl with electric mixer until smooth and changed in colour. Stir in sifted flours and cocoa, combined coffee and liqueur, chocolate and nuts; mix to a firm dough.
3 Gently knead dough on floured surface until smooth; divide dough in half. Shape each half into a 7cm x 20cm log. Place logs on greased large baking tray. Bake, uncovered, in moderate oven about 30 minutes or until firm. Cool on tray 15 minutes.
4 Using a serrated knife, cut logs on an angle into 5mm slices; place slices on baking trays. Bake in moderate oven 15 minutes or until both sides are dry and crisp; cool. Serve with coffee, if desired.

makes 50
tips Suitable to freeze This recipe can be made 2 weeks ahead.

swirled choc-almond biscotti

preparation time 25 minutes (plus refrigeration time)
cooking time 45 minutes (plus cooling time)

60g butter
1 cup (220g) caster sugar
1 teaspoon vanilla essence
3 eggs
2¼ cups (335g) plain flour
1 teaspoon baking powder
½ teaspoon bicarbonate
    of soda
1½ cups (240g) blanched
    almonds, chopped coarsely
¼ cup (25g) cocoa powder
½ cup (35g) plain flour, extra

1 Beat butter, sugar and essence in medium bowl until just combined. Add eggs, one at a time, beating until combined between additions. Stir in flour, baking powder, soda and nuts. Cover; refrigerate 1 hour.
2 Halve dough. Knead cocoa into one half of dough; shape into a 30cm log. Knead extra flour into remaining dough; shape into a 30cm log. Gently twist cocoa log and plain log together; place on greased oven tray. Bake, uncovered, in moderate oven about 45 minutes or until firm; cool on tray.
3 Using serrated knife cut log, diagonally, into 1cm slices. Place slices on ungreased oven trays.
4 Bake, uncovered, in moderately low oven about 15 minutes or until dry and crisp, turning halfway through cooking; cool on wire racks.

makes 25

coffee & hazelnut biscotti

preparation time 35 minutes (plus setting time)
cooking time 40 minutes (plus cooling time)

½ cup (110g) caster sugar
1 egg, beaten lightly
¾ cup (110g) plain flour
½ teaspoon baking powder
1 tablespoon espresso-style
    instant coffee
1 cup (150g) hazelnuts, toasted,
    chopped coarsely
100g dark chocolate, melted

1 Whisk sugar and egg together in medium bowl; stir in flour, baking powder and coffee. Stir in nuts; mix to a sticky dough. Using floured hands, roll into a 20cm log. Place on greased oven tray.
2 Bake, uncovered, in moderate oven about 25 minutes or until browned lightly and firm; cool on tray.
3 Using a serrated knife, cut log, diagonally, into 1cm slices. Place slices on ungreased oven tray.
4 Bake, uncovered, in moderately low oven about 15 minutes or until dry and crisp, turning halfway through cooking; cool on wire racks.
5 Spread chocolate over one cut side of each biscotti. Allow to set at room temperature.

makes 20

almond biscuits

preparation time 30 minutes cooking time 15 minutes (plus cooling time)

3 cups (375g) ground almonds
1 cup (220g) caster sugar
3 drops almond essence
3 egg whites, beaten lightly
1 cup (80g) flaked almonds

1 Preheat oven to moderate.
2 Combine ground almonds, sugar and essence in large bowl. Add egg whites; stir until mixture forms a firm paste.
3 Roll level tablespoons of the mixture into flaked almonds; roll into 8cm logs. Press on remaining almonds. Shape logs to form crescents; place on baking parchment-lined oven trays. Bake in moderate oven about 15 minutes or until browned lightly; cool on trays.

makes 25
tip Biscuits can be made a week ahead and are suitable to freeze.

vanilla thins

preparation time 20 minutes cooking time 5 minutes

1 vanilla pod
30g butter, softened
¼ cup (55g) caster sugar
1 egg white, beaten lightly
¼ cup (35g) plain flour

1 Preheat oven to moderately
hot (200°C/180°C fan-assisted).
Grease oven trays; line with
baking parchment.
2 Halve vanilla pod lengthways;
scrape seeds into medium bowl
with butter and sugar, discard
pod. Stir until combined, stir in
egg white and flour.
3 Spoon mixture into piping
bag fitted with 5mm plain tube.
Pipe 6cm-long strips (making
them slightly wider at both ends)
5cm apart on trays. Bake about
5 minutes or until edges are
browned lightly; cool biscuits
on trays.

makes 24

fudgy-wudgy chocolate cookies

preparation time 15 minutes **cooking time** 10 minutes
(plus cooling time)

125g butter, chopped
1 teaspoon vanilla essence
1¼ cups (275g) firmly packed brown sugar
1 egg
1 cup (150g) plain flour
¼ cup (35g) self-raising flour
1 teaspoon bicarbonate of soda
⅓ cup (35g) cocoa powder
½ cup (75g) raisins
¾ cup (110g) macadamia nuts, toasted, chopped coarsely
½ cup (95g) dark chocolate chips
75g dark chocolate, chopped coarsely

1 Preheat oven to moderate. Line three baking trays with baking
parchment.
2 Beat butter, essence, sugar and egg in medium bowl with
electric mixer until smooth. Stir in sifted flours, soda and cocoa
powder; stir in raisins, nuts and chocolate chips and chocolate.
3 Drop rounded tablespoons of mixture onto trays about 4cm
apart; press each with hand to flatten slightly.
4 Bake 10 minutes. Stand cookies on trays 5 minutes; transfer
to wire rack to cool.

makes 24
tips Cookies can be made up to one week ahead; store in an
airtight container.
Other nuts, such as walnuts or pecans, can be used instead of
macadamias.

chewy choc-chunk cookies

preparation time 25 minutes (plus refrigeration time)
cooking time 10 minutes per tray (plus cooling time)

2 eggs
1⅓ cups (295g) firmly packed brown sugar
1 teaspoon vanilla essence
1 cup (150g) plain flour
¾ cup (110g) self-raising flour
½ teaspoon bicarbonate of soda
½ cup (125ml) vegetable oil
1 cup (120g) coarsely chopped toasted pecans
¾ cup (120g) coarsely chopped raisins
150g dark chocolate, chopped coarsely
½ cup (95g) white chocolate chips

1 Preheat oven to moderately hot. Grease baking trays.
2 Beat eggs, sugar and essence in small bowl with electric mixer about 1 minute or until mixture becomes lighter in colour.
3 Stir in sifted dry ingredients then remaining ingredients (the mixture will be soft). Cover bowl; refrigerate 1 hour.
4 Roll heaped tablespoons of the mixture into balls; place onto trays about 6cm apart, flatten into 6cm rounds.
5 Bake about 10 minutes or until browned lightly. Stand cookies on trays 5 minutes; transfer to wire rack to cool.

makes 20

chocolate chip cookies

preparation time 15 minutes baking time 15 minutes

125g butter, softened
½ teaspoon vanilla essence
⅓ cup (75g) caster sugar
⅓ cup (75g) firmly packed brown sugar
1 egg
1 cup (150g) plain flour
½ teaspoon bicarbonate of soda
150g milk eating chocolate, chopped coarsely
½ cup (50g) walnuts, chopped coarsely

1 Preheat oven to moderate. Grease baking trays; line with baking parchment.
2 Beat butter, extract, sugars and egg in small bowl with electric mixer until smooth; do not overbeat. Transfer mixture to medium bowl; stir in sifted flour and soda then chocolate and nuts.
3 Drop level tablespoons of mixture onto trays 5cm apart. Bake about 15 minutes; cool cookies on trays.

makes 24

mocha cookies

preparation time 20 minutes cooking time 12 minutes

150g butter, softened
¾ cup (165g) firmly packed brown
    sugar
1 egg yolk
2 teaspoons instant coffee granules
1 tablespoon hot water
1½ cups (225g) plain flour
1 tablespoon cocoa powder
20 large chocolate buttons

1 Preheat oven to moderate.
Grease and line two baking trays
with baking parchment.
2 Beat butter, sugar, egg yolk
and combined coffee and water
in small bowl with electric mixer
until smooth. Transfer mixture
to large bowl; stir in sifted flour
and cocoa, in two batches.
Knead dough on floured surface
until smooth.
3 Roll level tablespoons of
mixture into balls; place 5cm
apart on trays, flatten slightly.
Press 1 chocolate button into
centre of each cookie; bake
about 12 minutes. Cool cookies
on trays.

makes 20

caramel chocolate cookies

preparation time 15 minutes cooking time 20 minutes

1 egg
⅔ cup (150g) firmly packed brown sugar
¼ cup (60ml) vegetable oil
½ cup (75g) plain flour
⅓ cup (50g) self-raising flour
¼ teaspoon bicarbonate of soda
100g dark chocolate, melted
250g chocolate caramel bar, broken into squares

1 Preheat oven to moderate. Lightly grease two oven trays.
2 Beat egg, sugar and oil in small bowl with electric mixer until mixture changes in colour. Stir in sifted dry ingredients and dark chocolate; stir until mixture becomes firm.
3 Centre one square of chocolate caramel on 1 heaped teaspoon chocolate mixture; roll into ball, enclosing caramel square. Place balls on prepared trays, allowing 6cm between each cookie; bake in moderate oven about 10 minutes. Stand cookies 5 minutes; transfer to wire rack to cool.

makes 24
tips One heaped teaspoon is equivalent to 3 level teaspoons.
Chocolate squares with strawberry or peppermint centres can be used instead of caramel squares.
Biscuit dough is suitable to freeze.

chocolate lace crisps

preparation time 25 minutes (plus refrigeration time)
cooking time 20 minutes

100g dark cooking chocolate, chopped coarsely
80g butter, chopped
1 cup (220g) caster sugar
1 egg, beaten lightly
1 cup (150g) plain flour
2 tablespoons cocoa powder
¼ teaspoon bicarbonate of soda
¼ cup (40g) icing sugar

1 Melt chocolate and butter in small saucepan over low heat.
Transfer to medium bowl.
2 Stir in caster sugar, egg and sifted flour, cocoa and soda.
Cover; refrigerate about 15 minutes or until mixture is firm
enough to handle.
3 Preheat oven to moderate. Grease baking trays; line with
baking parchment.
4 Roll level tablespoons of mixture into balls; roll each ball in
icing sugar, place on trays 8cm apart. Bake about 15 minutes;
cool crisps on trays.

makes 24

Chocolate heaven

choc-cherry cheesecake

preparation time 30 minutes (plus refrigeration time)
cooking time 50 minutes

125g plain chocolate biscuits
75g butter, melted
2 x 250g packets cream cheese, softened
⅓ cup (75g) caster sugar
2 eggs
200g dark chocolate, melted
3 x 50g dark chocolate Bounty bars, chopped coarsely
425g can pitted black cherries in syrup, drained

1 Grease 24cm springform tin.
2 Blend or process biscuits until mixture resembles fine breadcrumbs.
Add butter; process until just combined. Using one hand, press biscuit
mixture evenly over base of prepared tin. Cover; refrigerate about
30 minutes or until firm.
3 Preheat oven to moderate.
4 Meanwhile, beat cheese and sugar in medium bowl with electric mixer
until smooth; add eggs, one at a time, beating well between additions.
Gradually beat in chocolate; fold Bounty bars and cherries into mixture.
5 Place tin on oven tray. Spread cheesecake mixture into tin; bake in
moderate oven about 50 minutes or until set. Remove from oven; cool
to room temperature. Cover; refrigerate 3 hours or overnight.
6 Serve cheesecake decorated with chocolate roses, if desired.

chocolate roses To make chocolate roses, melt your choice of chocolate
then spread evenly over marble or a foil-covered surface. When chocolate is
almost set, drag ice-cream scoop over surface of chocolate to make roses.

serves 10

mars bar cheesecake

preparation time 30 minutes (plus refrigeration time)
cooking time 5 minutes

250g plain chocolate biscuits
150g butter, melted
2 tablespoons brown sugar
20g butter, extra
300ml whipping cream
50g milk chocolate, chopped finely

3 teaspoons gelatine
¼ cup (60ml) water
2 x 250g packets cream cheese, softened
½ cup (110g) caster sugar
3 x 60g Mars bars, chopped finely

1 Blend or process biscuits until mixture resembles fine breadcrumbs. Add butter; process until just combined. Using one hand, press biscuit mixture evenly over base and side of 20cm springform tin, cover; refrigerate about 30 minutes or until firm.

2 Meanwhile, combine brown sugar, extra butter and 2 tablespoons of the cream in small pan; stir over low heat, until sugar dissolves, to make butterscotch sauce.

3 Combine chocolate and another 2 tablespoons of the cream in another small pan; stir over low heat until chocolate melts.

4 Sprinkle gelatine over the water in small heatproof jug; stand jug in small saucepan of simmering water. Stir until gelatine dissolves; cool 5 minutes.

5 Beat cheese and caster sugar in medium bowl with electric mixer until smooth. Beat remaining cream in small bowl with electric mixer until soft peaks form. Stir slightly warm gelatine mixture into cheese mixture with Mars bars; fold in cream.

6 Pour half of the cheese mixture into prepared tin; drizzle half of the butterscotch and chocolate sauces over cheese mixture. Pull skewer backwards and forwards through mixture several times to create marbled effect. Repeat process with remaining cheese mixture and sauces. Cover cheesecake; refrigerate about 3 hours or until set.

serves 8

tips You can also melt the milk chocolate and cream in a microwave oven; cook on HIGH (100%) about 1 minute, stirring twice while cooking.

chocolate hazelnut self-saucing puddings

preparation time 15 minutes cooking time 25 minutes

½ cup (125ml) milk
40g dark chocolate, chopped coarsely
50g butter
⅓ cup (35g) cocoa powder
½ cup (75g) self-raising flour
¼ cup (25g) ground hazelnuts
⅓ cup (75g) caster sugar
⅔ cup (150g) firmly packed brown sugar
1 egg, beaten lightly
¾ cup (180ml) water
40g butter, chopped, extra
200g vanilla ice-cream

chocolate hazelnut sauce
½ cup (125ml) double cream
2 tablespoons brown sugar
50g dark chocolate, chopped finely
⅓ cup (110g) Nutella
1 tablespoon Frangelico liqueur

1 Preheat oven to moderate. Grease four 1-cup (250ml) ovenproof dishes.
2 Stir milk, chocolate, butter and half of the cocoa in small saucepan over low heat until smooth.
3 Combine flour, ground hazelnuts, caster sugar and half of the brown sugar in medium bowl. Add chocolate mixture and egg; stir until combined. Divide mixture among prepared dishes.
4 Stir the water, extra butter, remaining brown sugar and remaining cocoa in small saucepan over low heat until smooth. Pour hot mixture gently and evenly over puddings; bake puddings, uncovered, in moderate oven about 25 minutes. Stand 5 minutes; top with ice-cream then chocolate hazelnut sauce.

chocolate hazelnut sauce Combine cream and sugar in small saucepan. Bring to a boil; remove from heat. Add chocolate; stir until smooth. Add Nutella and liqueur; stir until smooth.

serves 4
tip This dessert is best served hot as the sauce is quickly absorbed by the puddings.

berries with white chocolate sauce

preparation time 10 minutes **cooking time** 5 minutes

½ cup (125ml) double cream
125g white chocolate, chopped finely
1 tablespoon Malibu liqueur
500g strawberries, quartered
300g blueberries

1 Bring cream to a boil in medium saucepan; remove from heat.
Add chocolate; stir until smooth. Stir in liqueur.
2 Serve warm sauce over berries.

serves 4

warm chocolate pavlovas

preparation time 5 minutes cooking time 35 minutes

2 egg whites
1⅓ cups (215g) icing sugar
⅓ cup (80ml) boiling water
1 tablespoon cocoa powder,
   sifted
500ml chocolate ice-cream

chocolate custard sauce
1 tablespoon cornflour
1 tablespoon cocoa powder,
   sifted
1 tablespoon caster sugar
1 cup (125ml) milk
2 egg yolks

1 Preheat oven to moderate.
Line large oven tray with baking
parchment.
2 Beat egg whites, icing sugar
and the water in small bowl with
electric mixer about 10 minutes
or until firm peaks form.
3 Fold sifted cocoa into
meringue. Drop six equal
amounts of mixture onto tray; use the back of a spoon to create well in
centre of mounds. Bake about 25 minutes or until firm to touch.
4 Meanwhile, make chocolate custard sauce.
5 Serve pavlovas straight from the oven, topped with ice-cream and sauce.

chocolate custard sauce Blend cornflour, cocoa and sugar with milk in small
saucepan. Stir in egg yolks. Stir over heat until sauce boils and thickens.

serves 4

chocolate jaffa tart

preparation time 30 minutes (plus refrigeration time)
cooking time 55 minutes

1½ cups (225g) plain flour
¼ cup (40g) icing sugar
125g chilled unsalted butter, chopped
2 egg yolks
2 teaspoons iced water, approximately
3 eggs
1 tablespoon finely grated orange rind
⅔ cup (160ml) whipping cream
¼ cup (165g) caster sugar

60g dark chocolate, melted
2 tablespoons cocoa powder
2 tablespoons Grand Marnier
140g dark chocolate, chopped coarsely, extra
¼ cup (60ml) whipping cream, extra
20 Ferrero Rocher chocolates, halved

1 Grease 24cm-round loose-based flan tin.

2 Blend or process flour, icing sugar and butter until crumbly. Add egg yolks and enough of the water to make ingredients just come together. Knead pastry on floured surface until smooth. Cover with cling film; refrigerate 30 minutes.

3 Roll pastry, between sheets of baking parchment, until large enough to line prepared tin; lift pastry into tin. Press into side; trim edge. Cover; refrigerate 30 minutes.

4 Preheat oven to moderately hot.

5 Cover pastry with baking parchment; fill with dried beans or rice. Place on oven tray; bake in moderately hot oven 10 minutes. Remove parchment and beans. Bake further 10 minutes or until pastry is browned lightly; cool.

6 Meanwhile, whisk eggs, rind, cream, caster sugar, chocolate, sifted cocoa powder and liqueur in medium bowl until combined.

7 Reduce oven temperature to moderate. Pour mixture into pastry case. Bake in moderate oven about 30 minutes or until filling is set; cool.

8 Place extra chocolate and extra cream in small saucepan; stir over low heat until smooth. Spread warm chocolate mixture over top of cold tart; refrigerate until set. Just before serving, decorate with Ferrero Rocher halves.

serves 8

black forest roulade

preparation time 20 minutes baking time 10 minutes

200g dark chocolate, chopped
   coarsely
¼ cup (60ml) hot water
1 teaspoon instant coffee powder
4 eggs, separated
½ cup (110g) caster sugar
1 tablespoon caster sugar, extra
½ cup (125ml) whipping cream
1 tablespoon kirsch

cherry filling
425g can pitted black
   cherries
3 teaspoons cornflour
1 tablespoon kirsch

1 Position oven shelves; preheat oven to moderate. Grease
25cm x 30cm swiss roll tin; line base with baking parchment.
2 Combine chocolate, water and coffee in large heatproof bowl;
sit bowl over saucepan of simmering water. Using wooden spoon,
stir until chocolate melts then immediately remove bowl from
pan to bench.
3 Beat egg yolks and sugar in small bowl with electric mixer until
thick and creamy; this will take about 5 minutes. Using large
metal spoon, fold egg mixture into warm chocolate mixture.
4 Beat egg whites in small bowl with electric mixer until soft
peaks form. Using metal spoon, gently fold egg whites into
chocolate mixture, in two batches. Spread mixture into prepared
tin. Bake in moderate oven about 10 minutes.
5 Meanwhile, place large sheet of baking parchment on board;
sprinkle with extra sugar. Turn cake onto sugared baking
parchment; carefully remove lining paper, cover cake loosely with
tea-towel. Cool cake to room temperature.
6 Beat cream and kirsch in small bowl with rotary or electric
mixer until firm peaks form. Spread cake evenly with cooled
cherry filling then spread kirsch cream over cherry mixture. Roll
cake from a long side, using paper to lift and guide the roll; place
on serving plate. Cover roll; refrigerate 30 minutes before
serving.

cherry filling Drain cherries, reserving ¼ cup (60ml) of syrup. Chop cherries coarsely. Using wooden spoon, blend cornflour and reserved syrup in small pan. Add cherries; stir over heat until mixture boils and thickens. Remove from heat, stir in kirsch; cover surface of mixture with cling film, cool to room temperature.

serves 6

tip It is vital to beat the egg yolk/sugar mixture until thick and to only beat the egg whites until soft peaks form. Overbeating will dry out the egg whites and make it difficult to fold them into the chocolate mixture.

raspberry & chocolate mousse trifle

preparation time 30 minutes (plus refrigeration time)

150g dark chocolate, chopped coarsely
½ cup (125ml) whipping cream
1 egg, separated
2 teaspoons caster sugar
85g packet raspberry jelly crystals
200g packaged chocolate sponge fingers (approximately 6)
¼ cup (60ml) coffee-flavoured liqueur
1 cup (135g) raspberries
300ml whipping cream, extra

1 Combine chocolate and cream in small saucepan; stir over heat, without boiling, until smooth. Remove from heat; whisk in egg yolk. Transfer to medium bowl.
2 Place egg white and sugar in small bowl; beat with electric mixer until sugar dissolves. Gently fold egg white mixture into chocolate mixture. Cover; refrigerate mousse 3 hours or overnight.
3 Meanwhile, make jelly according to manufacturer's instructions; refrigerate until jelly just begins to set.
4 Cut sponge fingers into 1.5cm slices. Place slices over base and around side of deep 2-litre (8 cup) large serving bowl; drizzle evenly with liqueur. Pour jelly over sponge fingers; refrigerate until jelly sets.
5 Sprinkle half of the raspberries over jelly; spread evenly with mousse. Top with whipped extra cream and remaining raspberries. Sprinkle with chocolate shavings, if desired.

serves 6
tips Mousse can be prepared up to 2 days ahead; trifle can be assembled 1 day ahead.
Frozen raspberries, thawed, can be substituted for the fresh raspberries.
In step 3, jelly should set to the same consistency as an unbeaten egg white.
Tia Maria, Kahlua and crème de caçao are all coffee-flavoured liqueurs; any one of them can be used in this recipe.

chocolate nougat frozen parfait

preparation time 20 minutes (plus freezing time)

2 cups (400g) ricotta cheese
½ cup (110g) caster sugar
300ml whipping cream
200g dark chocolate, melted
150g almond nougat, chopped finely

1 Line base and two long sides of 14cm x 21cm loaf tin with foil or baking parchment, extending over edge of sides.
2 Blend or process ricotta and sugar until smooth; transfer to medium bowl. Beat cream in small bowl with electric mixer until soft peaks form. Fold cream into ricotta mixture; fold in chocolate and nougat.
3 Spoon mixture into prepared tin. Cover with foil; freeze overnight or until firm.
4 Turn out of tin; cut into slices. Stand 10 minutes before serving, to allow it to soften slightly.
5 Serve sliced with raspberries, if desired.

serves 6
tips Chocolate suitable to microwave
This recipe is best made a day ahead.

coco-cherry ice-cream timbale

preparation time 10 minutes
(plus refrigeration time)
cooking time 2 minutes

2 litres (8 cups) good quality
   vanilla ice-cream
3 x 50g dark chocolate Bounty
   bars, chopped coarsely
1 cup (140g) caramelised
   almonds, chopped coarsely
50g glacé cherries, chopped
   coarsely
50g pink marshmallows, chopped
   coarsely
50g dark chocolate, chopped
   coarsely
pink food colouring
300ml double cream
100g white chocolate, chopped
   finely

1 Soften ice-cream in large bowl; stir in Bounty bars, nuts, cherries,
marshmallow, dark chocolate and enough colouring to tint the ice-cream
pink. Divide mixture among eight 1-cup (250ml) moulds. Cover with foil;
freeze 3 hours or overnight.
2 Place cream in small saucepan; bring to a boil. Remove from heat;
add white chocolate. Stir until chocolate melts.
3 Turn ice-cream timbales onto serving plates; drizzle with warm white
chocolate sauce.

serves 8

frozen mocha mousse

preparation time 1 hour (plus freezing and refrigeration time)

dark chocolate layer
**100g dark eating chocolate,
melted**
**2 teaspoons coffee-flavoured
liqueur**
2 eggs, separated
½ cup (125ml) whipping cream

milk chocolate layer
**100g milk eating chocolate,
melted**
**2 tablespoons coffee-flavoured
liqueur**
2 eggs, separated
½ cup (125ml) whipping cream

white chocolate layer
**120g white eating chocolate,
melted**
60g butter, melted
**2 teaspoons coffee-flavoured
liqueur**
3 eggs, separated
⅔ cup (160ml) whipping cream

nutty chocolate sauce
½ cup (165g) Nutella
¾ cup (180ml) whipping cream
**1 tablespoon coffee-flavoured
liqueur**

1 Line 14cm x 21cm loaf tin with
cling film.
2 To make dark chocolate layer,
combine chocolate, liqueur and egg
yolks in large bowl, stir until smooth.
Whip cream in small bowl until soft
peaks form, fold into chocolate
mixture. Beat egg whites in small
bowl until soft peaks form, fold into
chocolate mixture.
3 Pour dark chocolate mixture into
prepared tin; cover with foil, freeze
until firm.
4 Top with milk chocolate layer,
cover; freeze until firm.
5 Top with white chocolate layer,
cover; freeze until firm.
6 Turn mousse onto serving plate;
remove cling film. Slice mousse, serve
with nutty chocolate sauce.

milk chocolate layer Combine
chocolate, liqueur and egg yolks in
large bowl, stir until smooth. Whip
cream in small bowl until soft peaks
form, fold into chocolate mixture.
Beat egg whites in small bowl until
soft peaks form, fold into milk
chocolate mixture.

white chocolate layer Combine chocolate, butter, liqueur and egg yolks in large bowl, stir until smooth. Whip cream in small bowl until soft peaks form, fold into chocolate mixture. Beat egg whites in small bowl until soft peaks form, fold into white chocolate mixture.

nutty chocolate sauce Place Nutella in heatproof bowl, stir over hot water until pourable, gradually stir in cream and coffee liqueur; refrigerate until cool.

serves 10

chocolate heaven

mississippi mud cake

preparation time 25 minutes cooking time 1 hour 30 minutes

250g butter, chopped coarsely
150g dark chocolate, chopped coarsely
2 cups (440g) caster sugar
1 cup (250ml) hot water
⅓ cup (80ml) coffee liqueur
1 tablespoon instant coffee powder
1½ cups (225g) plain flour
¼ cup (35g) self-raising flour
¼ cup (25g) cocoa powder
2 eggs, beaten lightly

1 Position oven shelves; preheat oven to moderately low. Grease deep 20cm-round cake tin; line base and side with baking parchment.
2 Combine butter, chocolate, sugar, the water, liqueur and coffee powder in medium saucepan. Using wooden spoon, stir over low heat until chocolate melts.
3 Transfer mixture to large bowl; cool 15 minutes. Whisk in combined sifted flours and cocoa, then eggs. Pour mixture into prepared tin.
4 Bake cake in moderately low oven about 1½ hours. Stand cake for 30 minutes then turn onto wire rack, turn cake top-side up to cool.

serves 16
tips Any coffee or chocolate-flavoured liqueur (Tia Maria, Kahlua or Crème de Cacao) can be used in this recipe.
Cover cake loosely with foil about halfway through the baking time if it starts to overbrown.
The melted chocolate mixture can be made in a large microwave-safe bowl on HIGH (100%) in the microwave oven for about 3 minutes, pausing to stir four times during cooking time.
Cake will keep for up to 1 week if placed in an airtight container in the refrigerator Cake can be frozen for up to 3 months.

choc-cherry mud cake

preparation time 35 minutes (plus standing time) **cooking time** 2 hours

250g unsalted butter, chopped
1 tablespoon instant coffee powder
1⅔ cups (400ml) coconut milk
200g dark chocolate, chopped coarsely
2 cups (440g) caster sugar
¾ cup (110g) self-raising flour
1 cup (150g) plain flour
¼ cup (25g) cocoa powder
2 eggs
2 teaspoons vanilla essence
3 x 50g dark chocolate Bounty bars, chopped coarsely
50g glacé cherries, chopped
200g dark chocolate, chopped coarsely, extra
125g unsalted butter, chopped, extra

chocolate panels
300g dark chocolate, chopped
1 teaspoon vegetable oil

1 Preheat oven to low. Grease deep 22cm-round cake tin; line base and side with baking parchment.
2 Melt butter in large saucepan; add coffee, coconut milk, chocolate and sugar. Stir over heat until chocolate melts and sugar dissolves; cool to room temperature.
3 Whisk in sifted dry ingredients, then eggs and essence; stir in half the Bounty bars and cherries. Pour mixture into prepared tin. Top with remaining Bounty bars and cherries; bake in low oven about 1¾ hours. Stand cake 10 minutes; turn, top-side up, onto wire rack to cool.
4 Combine extra chocolate and extra butter in small saucepan; stir over low heat until smooth. Refrigerate until mixture is of spreadable consistency.
5 Spread chocolate mixture all over cake; place chocolate panels around side of cake. Serve with whipped cream, if desired.

chocolate panels Combine chocolate and oil in medium heatproof bowl; stir over medium saucepan of simmering water until smooth. Cut two 6cm x 50cm strips of baking parchment. Spread chocolate evenly over strips; lift strips to allow chocolate to drip off paper. Allow chocolate to set, then, using ruler as guide, cut chocolate into 4cm panels with sharp knife. Carefully peel away baking parchment.

serves 12

tip You can also melt the chocolate for the chocolate panels in a microwave oven; cook on MEDIUM (55%) about 1 minute, stirring twice during cooking. Stir in the oil once the chocolate has melted.

glossary

almonds
blanched brown skins removed.
caramelised toffee-coated nuts.
flaked paper-thin slices.
ground nuts are powdered to a flour-like texture.
aniseed also called anise; the licorice-flavoured seeds of the anise plant.
baking powder a raising agent: 1 teaspoon cream of tartar plus ½ teaspoon bicarbonate of soda is equal to 2 teaspoons baking powder.
bicarbonate of soda also known as baking soda.
bounty bar chocolate covered coconut bar, available in milk or plain chocolate
cardamom can be bought in pod, seed or ground form. Has a distinctive, aromatic, rich flavour.
chocolate made of cocoa liquor, cocoa butter and sugar; available in milk, white and dark. Use a high-quality eating variety.
chips these small morsels hold their shape in baking and are ideal as a cake decoration.
cocoa powder unsweetened, dried, roasted then ground cocoa beans.
coconut milk from the second pressing grated coconut flesh.
coffee-flavoured liqueur Tia Maria, Kahlua or any generic brand.
cointreau a clear French liqueur, orange-flavoured brandy.
cornflour also known as cornstarch; used as a thickening agent in cooking.
cream, whipping (minimum fat content 35%); cream containing a thickener.

cream cheese (minimum fat content 33%) soft cow's milk cheese.
ferrero rocher a commercial sweet made from hazelnuts and milk chocolate.
flour
plain an all-purpose flour, made from wheat.
self-raising an all-purpose flour mixed with baking powder in the proportion of 1 cup flour to 2 teaspoons baking powder.
frangelico a hazelnut-flavoured liqueur.
gelatine we used powdered gelatine; also available in sheets called leaf gelatine.
glacé cherries cherries cooked in heavy sugar syrup then dried.
golden syrup a by-product of refined sugarcane.
grand marnier a brandy-based, orange-flavoured liqueur.
hazelnuts also known as filberts; plump, grape-size, rich, sweet nut with a brown inedible skin.
ground the nut is roasted then powdered to a flour-like texture for use in baking.
ice-cream we used an ice-cream with 5g of fat per 100ml.
kirsch cherry-based liqueur.
macadamias a rich and buttery nut native to the USA; store in the refrigerator due to high oil content.
malibu brand name of a rum-based coconut liqueur.
mars bar chocolate bar containing soft nougat and caramel.
marshmallows pink and white; made from sugar, glucose, gelatine and cornflour.

milk we used full-cream homogenised milk unless otherwise specified.
nutella a chocolate-hazelnut spread.
pecans golden-brown, buttery and rich nuts.
pistachios pale green, delicately flavoured nut inside hard off-white shells.
ricotta soft, white, cow-milk cheese. A sweet, moist cheese with a slightly grainy texture and a fat content of around 8.5 per cent.
starfruit pale green or yellow in colour, with a clean, crisp texture. Flavour may be sweet or sour, depending on the variety and when it was picked. There is no need to peel or deseed it and they're slow to discolour.
sugar
brown a soft, fine granulated sugar containing molasses to give its characteristic colour.
caster also known as superfine or finely granulated table sugar.
icing sugar also known as confectioners' sugar or powdered sugar; crushed granulated sugar
toblerone chocolate bar with chopped nuts and nougatine
vanilla
pod dried long, thin pod with tiny black seeds that impart a luscious vanilla flavour in baking and desserts.
essence distilled from the seeds of the vanilla pod; imitation vanilla extract is not a good substitute.
walnuts rich, crisp-textured nuts with crinkled surfaces and an astringent flavour.

conversion charts

MEASURES

The cup and spoon measurements used in this book are metric: one measuring cup holds approximately 250ml; one metric tablespoon holds 20ml; one metric teaspoon holds 5ml.

All cup and spoon measurements are level.

The most accurate way of measuring dry ingredients is to weigh them. When measuring liquids, use a clear glass or plastic jug with metric markings.

We use large eggs with an average weight of 60g.

WARNING This book may contain recipes for dishes made with raw or lightly cooked eggs. These should be avoided by vulnerable people such as pregnant and nursing mothers, invalids, the elderly, babies and young children.

DRY MEASURES

METRIC	IMPERIAL
15g	½oz
30g	1oz
60g	2oz
90g	3oz
125g	4oz (¼lb)
155g	5oz
185g	6oz
220g	7oz
250g	8oz (½lb)
280g	9oz
315g	10oz
345g	11oz
375g	12oz (¾lb)
410g	13oz
440g	14oz
470g	15oz
500g	16oz (1lb)
750g	24oz (1½lb)
1kg	32oz (2lb)

LIQUID MEASURES

METRIC	IMPERIAL
30ml	1 fl oz
60ml	2 fl oz
100ml	3 fl oz
125ml	4 fl oz
150ml	5 fl oz (¼ pint/1 gill)
190ml	6 fl oz
250ml	8 fl oz
300ml	10 fl oz (½ pint)
500ml	16 fl oz
600ml	20 fl oz (1 pint)
1000ml (1 litre)	1¾ pints

LENGTH MEASURES

METRIC	IMPERIAL
3mm	⅛in
6mm	¼in
1cm	½in
2cm	¾in
2.5cm	1in
5cm	2in
6cm	2½in
8cm	3in
10cm	4in
13cm	5in
15cm	6in
18cm	7in
20cm	8in
23cm	9in
25cm	10in
28cm	11in
30cm	12in (1ft)

OVEN TEMPERATURES

These oven temperatures are only a guide for conventional ovens. For fan-assisted ovens, check the manufacturer's manual.

	°C (CELSIUS)	°F (FAHRENHEIT)	GAS MARK
Very low	120	250	½
Low	150	275–300	1–2
Moderately low	160	325	3
Moderate	180	350–375	4–5
Moderately hot	200	400	6
Hot	220	425–450	7–8
Very hot	240	475	9

index